This Book
Belongs To:

How to use this coloring book:

Rule #1: Have fun. This book is meant to make you smile, laugh, & have a good time with friends. It's for the love of all things Kawaii!

Rule #2: You can scan and print individual page images for personal use so you can color an image more than once, or to share with friends. You're allowed to scan images for coloring digitally too. For extra durability, you can laminate your bookmark; it'll last longer!

Rule #3: Be creative and give finished works away as super fun gifts. To aid with cutting, use a ruler and a sharp knife to remove pages. Make sure you have an adult's help!

Rule #4: Please do not post uncolored pages on-line or sell any images for profit, colored or not. You are encouraged to show off your colored images as much as you want though, as well as show photos or video for book review purposes!

Rule #5: Refer to Rule #1 & enjoy!

*Kawaii:
−said like Hawaii, but with a "k" means "cute" in Japanese.

Fox &
Grasshopper

Sea Otters

Bats

Cuttlefish

Mantis

Betta Fish

Hummingbird

Alligator

Killer Whale & Narwhal

Cat

Llama & Alpaca

Tiger & Carp

Axolotl

Toucan

Frog & Tadpoles

Lemur

Moose

Dog

Parakeets

Pig

Hammerhead & Whale Shark

Panda

Elephant & Mouse

Penguins

Wolf & Lightning Bugs

Test Color Page

Use Upside Down or Rightside Up!